LATE VICTORIANS

Late Victorians

VINCENT COLISTRO

THE POETRY IMPRINT AT VÉHICULE PRESS

Published with the generous assistance of The Canada Council for the Arts and the Canada Book Fund of the Department of Canadian Heritage.

Funded by the Government of Canada
Financé par le gouvernement du Canada

Canada

Signal Editions Editor: Carmine Starnino

Cover design: David Drummond
Photo of the author by Dallas Yuan
Set in Filosofia and Minion by Simon
Printed by Marquis Book Printing Inc.

Dépôt légal, Library and Archives Canada and the Bibliothèque national du Québec, second trimester 2016.

Library and Archives Canada Cataloguing in Publication

Colistro, Vincent, author
Late victorians / Vincent Colistro.

Poems.
Issued in print and electronic formats.
ISBN 978-1-55065-440-0 (paperback). – ISBN 978-1-55065-446-2 (epub)

I. Title.

PS8605.O449L38 2016 C811'.6 C2015-907351-0

C2015-907352-9

Published by Véhicule Press, Montréal, Québec, Canada
www.vehiculepress.com

Distribution in Canada by LitDistCo
www.litdistco.ca

Distributed in the U.S. by Independent Publishers Group
www.ipgbook.com

Printed in Canada on FSC certified paper.

For Michelle, who told me to write this

CONTENTS

Remainder Rising

It rises.
Whole fleets of notion set forth
an underwhelming wave, and it rises.

The remains of each cupboard and the time it takes
to clear them of their utilities: the remains of flour and yeast
and sugar come together in a new ingenuity, and it rises.

Manifold, brisk Cartesian theaters play
comedies of a single stake, and it rises.
Spectators eat the cake. A new building of wax erects inside tissue
which is only aesthetically pleasing on cold days when it rises.

Whole fleets of notion smash against the background, smelling
conspicuously of acrylic and with too few limes
for the scurvied deckhands. And though the ocean ought to be able
to accommodate a few extra dead bodies—*yet* it rises!

The remains of each cupboard are a destructed cake
waiting to be instructed, and though the creator suppresses,
suppresses, suppressessesses, *yet* it rises!

The Cartesian theaters have, like, limitless
material from which they can cull,
and the living know that to gesture toward dying one must often deflate
in the second act, *yet* it rises!

Death is as far as the question of death
can be to its adequate answer, so it rises. Whole fleets of answers
so close but so bleared by the fog (or else that's smoke
boiling up from the unnatural resolution of those deckhands)

form an expression of stolidity or grief or jubilation
depending on your position (geographical/historical),
that just *can't,* say the spectators, be arranged fixedly, so it rises.

The whole loaded cupboard are remains inside of remains
inside of remains inside of (arguably, if you're following)
colossal remains, which have nothing to service except
the greatest remains of all, so—since it can't possibly get any smaller—it rises.

The Pacifist

I was only born into the world,
didn't invade it, didn't ransom it for a nicer one.
I feel this way entering buildings
too. I don't mean anything by it.

When I type, as I am now,
it's like the tiptoes of titmice. I take a sip
of water and take my time swallowing
it. It goes down nice.

I only look because I've got these two
open eyes without a thing to do. They're like two
yoga poses, frozen in their inhalations.
Women: they're not any invitation.

When I walk to the chagrin
of a thousand blades of grass, it's not
to win any races, but to pass from one
shadow to the next.

I was only falling down the stairs,
to say. I am only a ruined conduit, as it is.
People speak in the caverns of my
ears and I hear it out my door.

When I sleep my dark double
peels back like a black seal from his place
in the stars and beats me to a pulp.
Then when the morning wakes me,
I hate to say it,
I feel refreshed.

The Muse

Seeing as I have all the sex appeal of a sack of flour,
and seeing as you are all notes rung at once, an infinitely-
petaled flower,

I hope you'll take this pervert art
as currency going forward, in what I hope to be
the start

of a very serious relationship. As the saying goes:
I'd give all parts of me that function to spend three
minutes with your clothes.

Do you know the work of Fra Lente,
my mentor? He's hell-sent, the bat, was bent on me
learning to cook pasta al dente

before I could dive into holding a brush.
A necessary evil and best avoided by a babe as you, he
has a grippe-stricken chicken's posture, but the lush

had a point. Nothing in art
is more important than negotiating patience and vitality,
except choosing the right muse. Let's start.

Can I evoke you? Okay, I evoke
you. You just have to sit there, maybe drape over the lee
side of the balcony, the wind baffling your thin cloak,

tippling a grape drink, the grapes of your feet
the bottom bauble of a treble clef. You see, see?
Being a muse is easy. I'll stab this sheet

and you simply be. An artist cannot simply
be, like you can; he cleans the caked-on spittle of the men he
proceeds, washing their pimply

backs and colluding in their quick
deaths. This is, I trust, not too cryptic. A grimace I see
taking shape between your dolphin kick

cheeks. Do you know something I don't
about artsy fartsy fancy things? I keep trying unsuccessfully
to bag an ounce of beauty here. Won't

that robe show any sheerer, ride higher?
Come nearer. We picked a particularly
windless day; this ant-line of friars

filing to their font in the background
does the scene no favours, nor does your inability
to mirror in the heft of your chest the round

domes in that yonder square.
We can have something everlasting and free
of human misery if we only strip ourselves bare.

Only share, only include in the prix fixe
of being human every steaming plat, pear, filigreed
bed sheet, bodice; reject your politics.

Forget about heirs and airs.
A funeral for me can be
a funeral for you. Who cares

if others slouch toward death unsteady
when we have the chance to transcend our facility!
As for the sex stuff, we can discuss it when you're ready.

Adulthood

We Rick-rolled, we raised
pre-flop, we flapped our pool noodles
at each other's caboose.

Weird weather propelled us; the rice-
paper pages of an Asia-on-a-shoestring guide
fluttered in the basket of a moped ride;

a pawned Swatch bought us
blackouts, as above an egret spread its grand potential
in the basin of a foreign moon.

We tsk during sex, I ask during
the best part of the movie. We ride
seasick horses into our 30s,

disembarking from the sexy
voyage, the I-gave-you-my-best-years
argument around the dreaded bend.

We observe kale Tuesday, we
stink in the afternoon, and by the evening
drink a recap of the day.

I wink and the bed sheets need
washing. I think and the whole apartment
gets clean. I think a rustic's

life I'd like, pulling hairy carrots
from their life below metaphors, brewing
my beer that'll knock our friend out cold,

leave him asleep on our bosomy
couch, to dream of one day having what we've got,
linen curtains beyond which a dog

spins its leash on the barbecue pit,
reliving its youth around and around
and around.

The Young Tyrants

They were the likely, the pestilent ones,
whipping into the bonfire with abandon
any symbol that wasn't theirs,
any necktie or haircut or care.

When they swam they gagged and bobbed,
as though being cooked alive,
and yet remained unpitiable. They skidded
their warts off in the dirt and bled out

in the anthills. I can well
remember the lobes on their furious ears,
their foreheads like a bearded rock
amid some pumping loam, their

eyes, oh my god, one could've sworn they held
a horde of undersexed soldiers behind there.
To them the forest was warm and easy. In every
movement they made they betrayed a view

of this world one could call sadistic
solipsism. The fish they'd suffocated
in a clear bag, the younger one they'd stripped
of his only pubic hairs, the fear of god they'd somehow licensed

for their own dispensation. Knowing
perhaps something it takes too much out of the rest of us
to know. That God is a malicious one too, and doesn't frankly care
if we attach ourselves to anything, or grow.

Food

The amuse-bouche was water chestnuts and duck air.
The sous-chefs came out of the closet
for us, and their courage was as palatable

as a raspberry. An aniseed was broken open
in the other room, and our wine underwent a small
change (that being

its 42nd birthday and all); we applauded the wine for this
and, much to our surprise, our hands clapped up a micro-dust
that smelt of frozen celery and germs. A decoy

course was presented to us, throwing us for a loop.
It was served in a collapsible polyethylene house, and diverted
our attention just long enough for the ether to kick in.

After a few hours laughing and sharing secrets,
the appetizer arrived. It was dandelion greens with
a bear-tooth enamel vinaigrette, fried giblets and giblet foam

and two roasted hazelnuts. The horniness of the dishwashing staff
was beginning to move into the dining area, so the host wheeled
a pale eunuch through the dining room to equalize

the situation. The post-appetizer was a sound course.
Canary whistles and horse hooves clacking on a paved road. It was
meant to evoke jam and peanut butter, but my partner and I agreed

it was not sweet enough. For the main course, we were given each
a Swahili name and taught a kind of rural Nyanzan dialect, the better
to enjoy the goat meat, which was prepared simply, in a car fire.

Dessert was an edible concept. A kind of white chocolate mathematic
that was more befuddling the more you understood it. It was served
with an ouroboros-shaped tuile wafer, which repeatedly

consumed and created itself. On the cab ride home,
we passed a theatre playing old movies, and my partner
remarked: "it's a shame that we weren't given popcorn",

and indeed it was a shame.
It was a shame that the restaurant was real, and not
some old, old movie.

The Gift

I undid the ribbon on the gift-
box and it must have been a load
bearing ribbon because
the gift imploded. This is also
the nature of a secret, which
is something structural and
existent until it's revealed.
Not to say the gift was a secret
but it was dropped off at my door
while I was asleep, with a note
that read: "your holic".
Holic isn't a word as far as I—
or the online dictionary I use—
know, but it could be a contraction
of "alcoholic", or an attempt
at the adjectival form of "hole". Or
it could be the Bosphorus inlet of Haliç,
The Golden Horn. It just plumb
crumpled in front of me, leaving
nothing to attest for its entirety
but the cryptic note. The writer might've
stopped after making an error, either
by duress or apathy; maybe he/she
intended to write "your holiness...".
The extravagance of the bow
might rule out apathy.
There's a lady who's always
walking about the apartment
complex asking for a light, and she
calls me a saint when I offer.
That might explain the duress.
I think she's on something most

of the time. I've never seen
anything quite like it before, the density
of the imploded gift was so great,
it rolled off the table and fell through
the floorboards. I went to go check
on my downstairs neighbour, to see
if she was okay, and if she could
return my gift ball, but she wasn't home.
In fact, her apartment too had
imploded, as had the vacancy which
it left behind. Come to think of it,
my life is full of these instances.

The Drifting Queen Elizabeth

Of druids and sweetbrier or eglantine and other
English lore and symbology, I admit to knowing next to
a cod's breakfast—which is nothing, I presume.

The ship set out from a thousand nodding handkerchiefs
until it knitted into the meridian; a red-headed family
poured tears into a biscuit tin; the sun never set

upon the moving ship, nor a sense of marital fidelity
upon its crewmen. I volunteered out of an electric curiosity.
A poet some years my elder told me I'd lose

my way with these men, who sunbathe day and day,
and leave lasses on the shore confined within a tawdry, Southern
European manner of bemoaning absence.

He wasn't entirely wrong. They speak as if tryingto force
two different species of bird together in functioning copulation.
It's rubbing off. Wrecked by rime, the whale oil paint

shucked off the hull into a Dadaist mess of half limericks.
Cock fights of meaning and rum barrel races go on long after night's
light, long before the breakfasting of the cods. The waves

appear and disappear to be blue handkerchiefs,
beckoning and mourning, recursively. The drifting of the ship
has created a more passionate art than any

land-smart, flower patch scholar could ever shake
from the old tropes of love and loss and accomplishment—
it's as though we've mated a harpoon with an albatross.

Town Hall

On the disappearance of good family eateries in the area,
and their being replaced by "bar and grills" in which women

wear socks as dresses and men wear helmets as hair, by
A Concerned Citizen. On the upmarket Authentico Ee-taliano

import stores that have muscled out the dollar dives
and driven the real estate prices up over my head like a wedgie,

by An Outraged Cook St. Villager. On that Moloch temple
you call a Wal-Mart, which pretty much *ruined* my acid trip

and is threatening to ruin everything else, by A Tripped Out
But Nevertheless Genuinely Enraged Citizen. On the Zoning

Commission dolt who thought it'd be okay to approve an
All-night Dance Club with street frontage on a narrow street

with a cluster of high-density multi-dwellings, by A Fatigued
Downtowner. On whoever's using the Cordova Bay beach access

to lay their 15 non-commercial crab traps each night then
just leaving the under-regulation-size females beached and

bleached of all their colour so my dog thinks they're treats
and eats them and now he has gut worms, by There's a Vet Bill

Waiting for You, Asshole. On the Fisgard Sex Store's anal
bead advertisement, which put me in the position of having to

explain to my four year old daughter why she couldn't have it,
by An Angry and Embarrassed Father. On the proliferation of

Ghost Walk Tours through The Ross Bay Cemetery, often
attended by foreigners with Hubble-sized cameras who leave

garbage around the graves as though the deceased *somehow*
depreciate over time until they're indistinguishable from a trashcan,

by An eighth Generation Victorian. On the intrusion of honkey
cafés in Chinatown—which I might remind everyone is the oldest

in North America—and their insistence on holding "art" events
that disrupt the Oriental aesthetic of the strip, By a Cultured

Victorian. On the Death of the Homeless Newspaper, the only
one of the city's papers that can't just say 'Oh, well, why don't

we move to a blog format' and what that means for information
in the lowest classes, by A Caring Citizen. On the automation of the

city Parkades, with an initial capital cost of $500,000 saving an
optimistic $300,000 annually, but putting 36 people out of work,

11 of whom have already expressed interest in moving East for jobs,
so the City is essentially robbing itself of their patronage in a blatant

attempt to fob off precarious workers, causing unquantifiable loss
in revenue, as well as the loss of my brother Rick to the Alberta

oil fields, by A Someone Using Their Brain. On the libraries'
loss-of-privilege rules designed to stop people, most with mental

illnesses, from searching for pornography, which flagged me for
looking up *Naked Lunch*, by An Ashamed Metropolitanite. On that

massive meteor heading towards us, that no amount of meditation
or conflict resolution or environmental protection or public planning

or literature promotion seems to be able to stop, which scientists say
will be here before the end of the day, By—

Bus

I bought a bus pass from the Middle Eastern grocer on Fort Street
and some pomegranate extract and rosewater and Macedonian feta.

The grocer mentioned a cult of Jesus in Macedonia that only
worshipped His unopened side. The grocer mentioned abstinence

in a creamy way that disclosed perhaps more than was intended.
The bus was a kind of Chaucerian comedy. Stories of cuckolded

friends of friends, an urban legend about two lovers who ate each other,
leaving a perfect, satisfied void. The bus brushed against a low-slung

garry oak, and I sat up straight and closed my eyes. I thought
about the cult of Jesus some more. The ads above the windows

appeared as ciphers, circles in triangles, an overabundance of Vs.
Had this moment, or any moment, been hatcheted and conjured for me?

Where indeed was my permission to open and spill out onto the floor
of this Chaucerian bus, to *know* the floor? The theosophic

experience of selfhood struck me like a bumper, and I hurried off
at the next stop. There were no oaks. There were tall conifers policing

a wide-open field. *O P E N*, I commanded, but it didn't.
Each leaf of grass turned to me its darkened side.

One Nameless Vilanelle

for you

Do you remember how you fell, face first into the last half of
your day, the ice in your drink, a lousy metaphor for
your life? The TV was on in the next room. There was a chattering above,

as your landlord and your landlord's wife fell out of love.
There shone a sickly light from the neighbouring store.
Do you remember how you fell, face first into the last half of

the night? The red alarm-light enclosed you like a glove,
in sentinel warmth, interminable bloops that blinked before
your life. The TV was on in the next room. There was a chattering above

as your landlord and your landlord's wife fell back into love.
There fell a sickly dust from their second floor.
Do you remember how you fell, face first into the last half of

the morning: a picaresque romp, an improbable shove
out of bed. Instances, in which you can honestly adore
your life. The TV was on in the next room. There was a chattering above,

that you knew to be a pigeon, but took to be a dove.
And you didn't even have to: the wind blew open the door.
Do you remember how you fell, face first into the last half of
your life? The TV was on in the next room. There was a chattering above.

176,000 km

Brushed with skycaps and goats grazing millet,
cloth-like badlands, shaggy wheat fields, and nights warm

with revelry, drunkards seesawing chip trails, some stooping against
an edifice, some flat-out collapsed in piecemeal alleys, so perfectly

still: this is how I imagine the space between us, and all
in a matter of a second or two. And then I picture you

encircled by goat-men who are violently with you, and in
the afterstroke, I am violently without you. Then I begin

to divine the space between us with a new indignity: how the man
loved his dog less on the neighbour's side of the fence,

the pig-girls who pulled me west by southwest, and made me thick
off the land, the smoke-pulled moths along the zodiac, fabric tongues

sweeping up the walls of an abandoned cryaway for widows
of the Spanish influenza, their wails. (Is there nothing new,

except the sensation of eternity, that isn't grafted?) The average
brain unraveled can travel up to 176,000 km—past that

is who-knows-what. The brain does all the loving,
and mine is road-worn, rot-shod

and gull-throated, sheened as a fly's back.
All I can do, traveling on the chimera's hump to find you,

is fail and fail and fail, move soil around to make new life,
in the hopes that I'll fail towards you.

The Love Song

Spoonsful of tenderness, spoonsful of anguish.
Someway measurements seem unable to predict an outcome.
Some can pour years into being funnier.

The bus is a moveable bunker, according to some.
Some can sleep unabated on the bus's seats.
Buses full of glances, buses full of private chortles.

Some lean from their seats at the drop of a secret,
but secrets vanish the moment they are uttered.
I looked up, maybe I am a secret.

Maybe I pour tenderness into something bottomless.
I think of anguish as when a bus first ducks underground
and suddenly, in the window, all you're left to look at is yourself.

Regathering

I searched everywhere in the back-
scapes of my life—through the backlogged paperwork,
the back of the topmost cupboard, the backs of old books—
to find my heart. I think I lost it

this time last year. I'd given up on it all. Allowed
mortality to piggyback onto everything, blowing the roof off what
I'd built. Why try, I thought? And here

the computer exacted an ounce of my heart,
and there a drink in the afternoon took some of it; the lion's
share was carved up by sleep and meted

to the various wishes my body made
when I wasn't around. My heart was scattered. It would be
near impossible to gather it all back. Michelle watched
as I travelled the apartment like a streetcar at night—as vacant
and vulgarly lit.

She hugged me to bed, cupped her life,
her workaday problems around mine and held them aloft. She sung
such elegant music. I searched the back-scapes,

thinking the shards of my heart would have dumbly
fallen somewhere. I tried to find it, actually, because
there have been a few deaths around me recently
and I could really use my heart. I did find it, too. Quite

by accident. I'd given up on getting it back, when I crawled
into bed and Michelle flung a half-asleep arm
around me. And there it was, gathered. I have to give
the little bastard credit, my heart, it knows how to get home.

Occasional Poem

Michelle exists, Japan exists, dogs exist
therefore I'll never commit suicide,

therefore all the mutt-dun lamps leading
east into town, casting doubt on the pleats

of my new pants, freeze as we saunter
past. What terrifying eyes in the window

of the fudge shop they blue. Surely sushi
glistens in Borneo, as sure as I am sheep

bah'd for Stalin once or twice, when in his
quaint Georgia town they ate of brassicas.

I try my schtick for Michelle, the one where
I'm a vampire cosplaying a Midwestern boy

but the boy betrays my own indignance
I feel being me. Let me get born a lover

of the outdoors, hey, if only for a while.
I shake a weighty willow for its five dollar bill

and the bill falls, in Fall, and buys us bus fare.
I can take us where our friend flew off the handle

one night and declared her life a mulligan,
adored a world un-her and unaware

she herself lost a good one that day.
I wouldn't for all the plum flowers in Chinatown

do it, not for the night bus to the end
of the night, not for the fuss I cause you

on occasion. It was here, I was so bashful
holding the world in your breast I turned

the radio full blast. As if all experience could
coincide to make us less and more alive.

Leisure

With no one to properly apply the tourniquet, he afforded himself
the rare opportunity to just bleed everywhere. On the bed skirt,
the garlic bowl, the painting of a smudge that could be a farmer,
the—the everywhere.

Blood became as a necessary aesthetic embellishment: the stucco
for example. Then it began to appear functional, as grouting.
Its copiousness sort of normalized it, so he sat in his chair and began
to read amid it.

Soon after, his wife came home, aghast of course, but he assured her
that the blood had probably always been there, that she should fix herself
a drink or a tomato sandwich and unwind a little bit.
Being in no mood

to argue with him, she obliged. It *was* glamorous. And it empowered her.
So the two sat on the sofa and shared little stories about their childhood
vacations, their soft inaccuracies, each with its own
twiggy architecture

until the man could no longer keep his eyes open. He died of course.
In the morning, life clicked back into its old position, and the woman
spent the day crying on the phone with her sister, then the police,
then the cleaners.

Betterment

With my juicer I knew I'd be better,
so diligently I juiced, until my pantry was naught but empty fibres.
I saw the pounds

fly off, their dense
webbings of fat expanded and they achieved flight—each
like a different bird of paradise.

I ate raw, as budding and zygotic
as nature offered, and my biceps regressed into the unripe avocadoes
of adolescence. I was the one on website banners

doctors hated, I was archangelically
wise and non-sexual, with Purell breath and pink affection,
a drama teacher. I shaved the trauma off my chest.

I knew I could transform into a broth-like
summer for the suffering teenage soul, could light up
a room, could herald our at-rest, be the half-

and-half in our tea. My genitals softened away,
like kitchen paper under the faucet, as my hair
grew in a concentrated beach atop the Indian Ocean

of my forehead. My bodily functions stopped.
I was Audubon's birds, was Ibn Tufail's dead gazelle of reason,
with a half-pipe sternum fusing two musical instruments.

When the city saw me for what I'd become,
the adults blenched and the children ran toward me. They did so
in their dawdling way, and the time it took for them to reach
my feet was Utopian.

The Prophets

The prophets evolved with the times,
pissed off and moving refrigerators

from an old man's loft. They had in the olden days
a malicious god who stalked and stomped

their pulses rotten. They called laughing bones
from the sand and were answered. The prophets grew

out of their naivety though. They're keen to slide their fingers
in His valley, His valley's rattlesnakes, His son. The sun

evolved in its slow way to set up a reflection
in umpteen windows, teens, chubby-naveled, soaking

the last bucolic ice-cubes of youth in their fountain colas.
The prophets laugh at indolence, though they themselves

ease into day's end as into a bottled lager, blowing
steam forth and saying, confident, we've revolved,

blowing through sick braces into a game cartridge
which, with a strapped right hand, can take over the world

it creates. They're all too aware of the homonym profits, scoff
when it's brought up, bluffing their online poker hand and
stoking—

no, not the flame—the phone that's charging in the other room.
God's calling, seeing if we're a party worth attending.

The Big One

When the Big One came,
the city's activists were on Parliament lawn
fixed in a mosaic saying *Save our Oceans.*

By the time it was through,
the mosaic read *Orca ova ensues.*
It carried Poe

from the wax museum, planted
him in Queen Elizabeth's arms. The ocean
flew fish-jets, seaweed streamers, feted

by the streetlamps bursting,
the bakeries and flour bombs. The pizza
people ordered had all the wrong

toppings, the theatres filled
with ducklings, the mall lost a decent amount
of money. Single origin coffee

brewed in the mighty tsunami,
staining the city's supply of chinos.
The surrealists wrote realism,

the realists surrealism, without
even betraying their aesthetic. Artists sold
umbrellas. Because *acting is reacting*

the actors quaked counter-
rhythmically, which they said was good
for empathy. The Big One

carried on for days without relenting,
taking people's wallets and giving people hiccups,
before, a week after starting, stopping

flatly. It would've been hell
to put it all back together, so we left it
jumbled. Went to our new jobs,

our new families, finding hope
on the rubble of a crumpled church,
whose gospel was transformation.

Damming

Rock after
rock, leg-like logs
the ocean had

petrified,
we stacked our
stock and milled
shells and sand
grout at our wit's

end; couldn't
keep the water
from, like a waking
beast, knuckling
itself

up, rising
over our redoubts.
I hear you shot
a bear recently,
have been

researching
the Illuminati
in a cabin up north.
This is what
I do.

Pomp On Wharf Street

Baked kids snicker over steak dinners
at the Stomp and Spit Pub on Tits-Up Street.

I feel like a cop on his beat, thanks
to a sheep-horn club I bought the pawnshop called

a shofar. A gauze-shod bouncer stanches
the entrance of The Ventricle Club. I look

like a vigilante from afar. Racially charged phone
poles show pictures of a missing job. Car after

Italian car. Baked Ziti graffiti on Vito's World
Famous, where frosh rattle lamesauce off like it's

a vicious insult. I have Band-Aids on from smoking
bees out of an arthritic Portuguese woman's tree

for ten dollars and a sausage coil, so I look
like a brawler. Gamers smoke on Zorba

the Geek's stoop, talking in a croupy basso,
all watching as I pass badassedly across

the halogen scraped street. The linalool smell
of marine-coloured hair gel clouds the sidewalk

by Tongue Lounge. The ladies swoon
like cartoon flowers when a stench comes around

and you can almost hear the men's grapes hole back up
in their prepubescent hiding place.

I have a face that only their mother could love.
I part the scrum of a bus line like a Mad Max Moses

leading his chosen coat-tail out of Little
Egypt. You can hear it in the garbage cyclones,

there's a case of routineness going around. I feel like
a terrible rain, like I just blew in from a meaner town.

Acting

In plays I have eaten the poison biscuit,
laughed in makeup at the chain of accolades.
I have been reviewed, a half-dozen times,

and not been found wanting. Nightly,
I break open as a woman and watch myself
like a man. My ascot askew and foam accruing

at the corners of my mouth. A song
is but half my work. A poem but a quarter, reasonably.
Mine Viscount says that upon the stage I am as naked

and horrific as a bald horse, my pheromones as palpable
as mulled wine. Mine Viscount is generous and odourless.
He presented me once a month's worth of elk meat, having

shot the poor thing. I was anemic then and losing sleep,
but my art, and mine Viscount's generosity, kept me healthy.
O, ineffable warrens of human nature, allow me to be

your muse, your skulking apparition, your logic.
Allow mine Viscount to ride in the front seat of our chariot
for three and wax inconsistently about the death

of the written word, the androgynous candles and the sound
of a semi-hollow stage, upon which one wrestles the dust. In plays,
I have floated into chambers and bemoaned the death

of one busty woman or another, drank for hours
at the Jewish cemetery, waiting for the morning *Times*
to be delivered to the gas station across the road.

I have married mine Viscount's daughter and deflowered
his son. I have squandered my money on funny masks. Beaks
of flightless birds do nightly peck my eyes out, in this

one recurring dream where I sell my clothes for a daughter, who rejects
my nakedness, and I'm left to hang by my lats in a black forest,
where nature devours me, and I listen in horror.

Late Victorians

M.C.

Thanks, um, everyone for coming. I know it's Christmas eve, and…

(At RISE, the GALLERY comes alive with variegated, variform FACES, folks waving in and out of chats on ekstasis, pimp informants, terrorism in Late Victorian architecture, etc. The space is massive and umbral, how a bug might see the world inside a sheer-curtained bed. VINCENT, 19½, works the bar. His DOUBLE, in a white Kaftan, a kind of celestial narrator, sits cross-legged in the rafters.)

VINCENT'S DOUBLE *aside*

There I am, a thin pistil of a thing. Already well into drunkenness's miry country, having mulled and drank the wine in equal measure. I was changing into more comfortable shoes, when the M.C. took his place, and gave me my cue.

M.C

Donations can go in the can marked "CanLit Can". Macy, I believe there used to be ragout in there?

VINCENT'S DOUBLE *aside*

I gave the poet, who was hiding behind an art installation, his five minutes. He nodded back with this distant dispassion, like a military painting from the 18th Century, which I probably didn't deserve.

(The BIG GUNS shoot the shit around a table selling the POET's books. A monochrome 1970s cover; a daguerreotype wagon on his 1986 award winner; a Matissian sketch on his 1993 selected, etc., all forming a u-shape around his latest, a lacquered black, thin-as-a-zine book with two spangled headlights dead centre. The book is irradiant, twinkling even!)

VINCENT'S DOUBLE *aside*

I served Ernesto Palvo a blended red wine and he exclaimed, cryptically of course, it was the most exquisite beef soup he'd ever tasted.

(The POET continues to lurk in the shadows. His eyes are two yellow pendulums. The art installation switches pivots and a lever which holds a beaker of red dye tilts, mixing it with a blue beaker to make a sultanate purple, backlit by a Fresnel lantern in the talons of a taxidermy falcon.)

M.C.

His collections include: *Martial Art: A Collection of Short Stances*; *Guzzle*; *I Awoke and a Raven*; *A Daypack for Hades*; *Jakaltek Blow Darts*; and most recently a long poem entitled—

(A few interrupted conversations waddle gaily to their chairs. The POET pushes away from the wall to announce his taking of the microphone and a lecture-hall hush draws the crowd from its mirth.)

POET

Thanks Philip. Thanks everyone too for abandoning your families (Laughter). And let's not forget Jane, who gave us the... I don't have my glasses... falcon? I'm going to read a short—well—extended elegy, *Late Victorians*, which, uh, among other things, is the product of a lot of thought about memorials. The, uh, memorial impulse...

(The front row consists of: TOM PAPER, BILL RICKEY, HELENA BETHUNE, E. K. QUINN, ERIN SHANNON, PATIENCE BELL, IVAN IVANOVITCH, EDISON HALL, BARRY TOMLIN, ERNESTO PALVO, DR. DELAROUGE, DR. CORTES, JOHN DUNN, SAMANTHA COLE, KULDEEP THANDI and five WELL-DRESSED UNDERGRADS)

POET

I was reading a letter, an Essex ironworker, like one of Ruskin's, who'd taught herself to read and write. She had the most morbid sense of humour, dedicating pages of barely legible script to a marionette play she was writing, to be performed by dead rats in bustles or frock coats. Here. I have—somewhere—ah, I have a copy. Her name was Hester and she wrote to *whom it may concern*.

M.C

Macy, this isn't the right can.

POET

Whole lineages she penned, see. Love triangles, mistaken identities. In one notable subplot, a young earl's daughter trades her sight to a Spanish warlock for the chance to find true love. True to her fate, she falls in love with a lamppost.

VINCENT'S DOUBLE

As if a ghost ship passing, a group of carollers outside singing *Good King Wenceslas…*

POET

Hester hastens to add it was a handsome lamppost…. Vernales in omnibus, imitantur mores (Laughter) Ahem. Then later in the letter, Hester complains of dizzy spells and poor vision and malaise. *No*, you think as you read it. No, it couldn't happen. But the long letter ends. So old and obvious, yet so abrupt. I found myself sick, as though I'd lost a daughter. Course my father was battling cancer at the time. May we…

(A stanza's worth of silence is observed for PAPER SR., who'd done a lot in his day for free verse.)

POET

"lateral, clavicle, acromion, / the pills of her spinal column / hunch into such extra- / natural designs / the kind of balled up / grief we see in handkerchiefs, / the operas of bizet / or russian ballets"

VINCENT'S DOUBLE *aside*

I didn't blame The Poet for his impoliteness. A celebrity's got to keep their particularities fixed on a broad and therefore distant point.

(Outside the arched windows, snow falls timorously through the slats of street- and traffic lights as the wind dies down. It holds a portion of THE AUDIENCE's attention before they remember that art, and probably suffering, is taking place in front of them. They correct their gaze, following the *hmm*'s and nods of the rest.)

POET

"capsule or flagellum. corpus / or portio. no cri de coeur / in this archipelago / of sorrows seems enough / and so we attempt to build a raft."

VINCENT'S DOUBLE *aside*

A crowd, on the other hand, generalizes itself upon a central point, which makes its *hmm*'s sort of mawkish.

POET

"but thousands of years / winding the tape /deck back / an errand I shared / with him as he plumbed"

VINCENT

Three sheets to the wind!
(he sits down next to Michelle)

VINCENT'S DOUBLE *aside*

Ah! That was the expression on the tip of my mind. I felt like his book, as a gust passed through. It seemed like the whole of humankind was in the room. Michelle stroked my corduroys.

(In the second row: STUART KITCHENER, DOMINIC AGROPINTO, NICAL TRUMAN, BEATRIX ISHERWOOD, PHILIP FUENTES, JANE G. XIANG, LOUISE NIEDERMAYER WEST, ROB SOMERVILLE, NESBITT BELCHER, R. T. WALSH, HOMER CHO, nine WELL-DRESSED UNDERGRADS and two MFA CANDIDATES IN SCREEN-WRITING.)

VINCENT'S DOUBLE *aside*

My mind itself chortled!

POET

"tom who has drawers / for his grief that click /shut and swallow / the absence and i / drove down route 8 // drunk off the remains of our father's / liquor cabinet / as hester's marionettes played /a stadium of dead voices / briefly vivifying"

VINCENT'S DOUBLE *aside*

But watch now! This is when it stopped. When it all started. What little of the poem made its way through… It held me as though I was some intricate newborn bird—

POET

"you could come back / as a tape deck, you / could come back as a horn / ashen and afloat / you could…"

VINCENT'S DOUBLE *aside*

In danger, with every webbed pump, of rupturing what fine unfortunate life had been afforded me. I can't remember if I wept or if I wanted to weep and couldn't—

POET

"as a middle distance / alighting from no single desire / to have you back..."

VINCENT'S DOUBLE *aside*

Internalization is so much like a pinball machine, with its buckets and causeways and strobing lights. But I do recall shivering and the lights anointing the lines on Michelle's hand, which opened as I stretched my knee to find space for whatever love or understanding was passing through my body, through my toes.

(In the third row: sixteen FACES glow like headlights, rimmed by the most spectacular exhaust.)

Direction

All told, turning all on their heels
like circuit breakers, it took a cracked second
for everyone to become my actors. I was bored
during an electric storm, and a black hole opened
into a director's cone. The shining storefronts

and stalled streetcars looked lonesome, relegated
to props. I ordered a man in a smoking jacket to read the papers,
thwack once the front page and huff. It sure worked. I yelled
for a woman to sneeze her glasses askew. I called
for bureaucracy everywhere. Soon love,

lectures, films set in the French Alps all became my creation.
Dollar store prices, hypochondria, guitar lessons,
both sides of the abortion debate, cake-making,
bath-time, local colour—

me. Every subjugation too! No, I hadn't planned this
well. Every senseless death and every quiet afternoon was mine.
I could no longer mean well. My relationships were relationships
with myself. I'd shout such hurtful things at me, and in return
I'd shout such hurtful things. I longed for the life

I had before, peopled and frightening. I went to see
an old movie, but even that was of no consolation: I could see
my hand pressing Bergman's back onto the plane. When I woke up
it was nearing summer and I was nearing thirty. I took the advice
of a friend and flew to the coast for some fresh air.

Close-Up Magic

I could feel his heart beat my cards
from their suits. Misdirection

in his lapel burned like two tall torches.
I followed his knuckles, rows of oak

barrels to where his wine poured
clear and even in the cup. The ball

his eye became, the cash machine
his ear. He heard my incredulity

with open hands, my peace of mind
with a fist of feathers. My face was a jet stream

about his smooth thumbnail, and his thin,
sweet and callow jokes buoyed

above his realest magic trick: he saw
inside me, throwing away age, he sawed

a woman of perception. Maybe she's really
open and what spills out will be

the thing-in-itself, I think. It is as real
as the whole woman, each of these halves

of her, the one lighting a cigarette to see
and the other running from the light.

Magic

I built a house out of hocuses and pocuses
out of mostly poofs and whisps that couldn't withstand
the winter. It was marginal, I mean,
the praise I received for my latest creations
the unwhirred earth and the laughing perfumes
the smocks of northern light and the tantric caves
but something is always lost
in conjuring. Something remains too,
anyways. After the last rafters were hocused
and the few remaining pipes pocused,
my lady could've sworn she heard a prowl
slumping in from the James Bay pier and I stood
disturbed at the row of light from the next room
(which was in fact light from a further room)
because knowledge itself seemed a hoax
The slumping thing bumped into lampposts

Oh, I conjured up that old playwright
The hours have become a sonnet
He said 'would you were but you are not
a shooting star. Of mine own I know"
or to that degree the margins withdrew
and I ate what can only be described
as the finest bowl of grapes.

Music

I dreamed I heard
a loose scree and Sherpa flute's
foreboding potpourri. The audience rose,
clapping the evening's pamphlet
to their other hand, misunderstanding
music. A tree dreamed

I was strumming
and vibrating out of the pell-mell.
Claps retracted and each
hand's back was then its front.
Wagner's gaze clipped a measure
before it resolved,

and everything,
every creature involved
in the dolorous fugue worked backwards
towards the source
of the sound.

When I came to,
I delighted in the midnight display:
the refrigerator's rumple and pssts of spray paint cans
making symbols I wouldn't know
until I walked outside
and saw what they had
to show me.

The Rainy Season

Upon his most marine body parts
sea flowers bloomed. He came to resemble
an anemone. This was mid-summer, and the rain
had lasted weeks, pelting the tired bees.
The for-sale signs and trees, post-ambition,
bathed. He dredged his chest of fine
asparaguses. Today, I'll learn German,
he said to the rain, and true to his word
he learned the German word for rain.
From the shell of his eardrum, he shook
an enterprising snail, who looked up at him
piteously, sharing a conundrum. I'm fine
the way I am, he said as a function of not
being fine, though not caring to change.
His non-sexuality hung like a lamp dropped
into a dark lake. The body he'd camped in
shivered with crane flies. Bloom became
him, as he stagnated in the water. I'm fine
the way I am, he said as a function of going
unnoticed. He could still hear the rain above,
tapping the surface of the water like so many
summer dancers. Jellyfish rowed
the length of his linen pants, linen shirt,
pomade: an underwater Gatsby, spying
love and looseness on the other side of
a great divide. Consider rain, he said
as a function of detaching himself, to no avail,
consider what the Germans call der Regen,
where a hard consonant remains like a tethered boat,
knocking opposite walls like an alley cat in heat,
combed with sour milk like a summer foal,
licked by its mother like the avant-garde,
sexless and in full bloom.

Moving Day

When I removed the piano I found
a small door in the wall's trim, pasted over with a puzzle box
like a wee foreclosed home,

so, naturally, I kicked it. Three
tines of light shot through, each a ramp
the curlicues of dust turned

into what looked to me like Arabic.
I got my eye up close to the opening and saw
seesaws of dead children inside,

flu-headed and grist-
brown, a truly revolting sight.
The piano backs onto the apartment

next to mine, so I paid
Mrs. Park a visit. Knuckle-deep
in a Cliff bar, not following

what the fuck I was trying to tell
her, she slammed the door, and I
could *feel* her eye

behind that peephole.
I returned to find the children rushing
back to class, past flotsam play-

grounds, half-sunk, to my—
wait, my!—old elementary school. Even
the creek was there, where Nick

Spiro had pissed on a crawfish.
I kicked again. Kicked. Puckered my lips
and wept. I was a creep. I stuck

my hand fully in
to find myself, but I must have been an
arm and an inch out of reach.

The grey glass shattered into cracked
wheat, the pocked paint job on the porticos
looked like plaquey teeth,

the dead ran their hands along the sidewalk
drawing chalk lines and medical symbols.
Their gums receded.

I spoke but no one listened.
I apologized later to Mrs. Park who anyhow
attempted to understand. She

admitted I look like a lover she once had
in Korea, that my face in certain lights has the same
burnt strands, like almost a middle eastern

script. It was terrifying to consider
that I hadn't moved my piano at all, merely played
a note that reminded me of my boyhood.

The Call

I fastened the chintzy hasp back over the jar I kept
my nickels stacked like an old flint wall in and forgot

all this nonsense about leaving home. I locked eyes
with a show, an older man in slack pajamas blowing

out a candlestick, shot a toe through my last pair of good
socks and forgot all this nonsense about leaving home.

I kissed the last airborne flap of tissue paper split
in twain at the ply-fold and not because I was crying;

I was trying to keep occupied while the TV tried to
sell me pale lager struck by surf, that I might buy some,

and forget all this nonsense about leaving home. The show's
main character realized his wrong-all-alongness, paid alms

to the homeless, while I remained static, skipped
to the nosebleed channels, finding static, forgot all this

nonsense about skipping channels. That was when the phone
rang, it was mid-afternoon. My friend's voice had this rusk

quality to it. He'd shot two ducks just straight from where
they flew, and was crying to me something about their ducklings,

some hateful, squeeze-toy wail they made, which made him
question every wretched decision his fingers helped in. What

could I do, you know? I blew the dust off my old flat cap
and kennel, flew out the front door to help him find them a home.

The Insiders

They were a mid-western, big-breasted family,
though the two men looked gaunt as greyhounds.

I watched them through the pub window, wanting
to be a picture in their shared digital camera, huddled

in a day-at-the-beach's damp sarong, making the surly
owner smile as he brought lemonade; an obvious

misuse of place doesn't faze a loving congregation. Then
I watched as a drunken tough-guy drifted in obliquely

and put his arms around one of the greyhound men,
nearly folding him in; nervousness struck them all smiling

with their eyes ranged down, as happens when beings are
torn between politesse and fear. The daughters adjusted

their strapless summer dresses up, as the dad
grabbed his cola to cheer the jackass at trunk-

level... Tension, through a stained window, translates
as just a big, grey dump of sadness. I peeled my coaster and looked

back. The drunk wandered off, back perhaps to his
fairytale cave, not before clapping the dad on the back,

leaving him to face his family, whose eyes were still fixed
on the floor, and say something like "strange guy, huh?"

It was tough thereafter to watch them, the way
they stayed inside themselves.

Panic Aquarium

Two tickets to see the pageant
of miniature terrorisms, as it's unveiled
and veiled again, dotted along the tubed corridor

connecting one emergency to another by way
of tanks. It's the glass that makes it emergent,
says the woman to my right, whose entertaining

foreign guests. They're too slow to photograph
the terrorisms as they swim in and out
of view, even though the one has fiddled with his aperture

for a good two minutes. It's thin, she explains,
selling them on the danger. And the tank is always overcrowded.
This makes them both majestic and appalling.

Some have translucent bodies and catch
a furious blue light in their ribs. Others are streaked
in intricate explosions. Some appear tattooed with capillaries.

They're so obviously hungry; I've never seen things so
hungry and awake. There's a rumour circulating that it's
the energy expended by them that lights their tanks, that

prints the tickets and sells them for profits that go
to the maintenance and continuation of the aquarium,
and that no one knows how this whole panic began.

Song

I was the elbow of my impulses, my own bee-fuzz
ear canals, when I myself opened to hear
the coming of song.

I was the indices of inventories of experiences
of aimless play, when a tornado ripped through me to hear
the coming of song.

I was my very own ocean's conch, hearing
my absences roar, when I pulled away to hear
the coming of song.

I walked a straight line to where the canal met
a few fishermen listing over, to reach in and hear
the coming of song.

With all the strength I'd left, I lifted the two logs
lodged into the footpath and walked through to hear
the coming of song.

I was footnoted in spider bites, the heat around my ankles
a red siren in my ears, which I flinched from to hear
the coming of song.

A one-two blow on my tea, I was as a red-faced Homeric cloud,
rerouting the homesick houseflies toward
the coming of song.

I was seated on the earth's knee, raining almonds
on the moss, around the jerky squirrels I joined to hear
the coming of song.

Two deaths as easily as a Tuesday went by, while I tapped
the thin marble with my shoe, expecting finally to hear
the coming of song.

To say I waited an eternity is a small
overstatement, for the song did finally come. I was old
as I was smooth,

I was pottery-like with inner lights, and I resembled the song
in all but its superficialities. We met cordially, like two
opposing generals

from a war no one really remembers.

The Asterisks

A tizzy of asterisks, demarcating like piranhas, leaving
the subject skeletal and still clacking.

Constellations of asterisks, sentient in the afterglow. Republics
of asterisk band and disband against the kleptocratic grammatical

magistrates. In a dream, asterisks are in the jungle, on every tree.
Scarier still, asterisks are on every leaf. Foreign,

mercantile tables and measurements
wind the veins and spines of the bracts. Oof,

say some asterisks, Ech, say others. Erp, a few.
The open fields seem uninhabited by asterisks until

one bothers using an electron microscope: Lucretian asterisks.
Epicurean asterisks. I feed my family black pepper asterisk.

I tried practicing Buddhism, but suspect enlightenment is
nothing more than an inescapable asterisk, an octopus asterisk,

the onomastic kraken of asterisk. They sit underneath
the universe, parochial and grandiloquent. Bombastic asterisks.

I tried practicing solipsism, but found an equal number of internal
asterisks. I could try dying, which would no doubt solve the problem,

but I have good things lined up—death is not a feasible or alluring option,
not over something like asterisks.*

*And even if I did off myself, my epitaph would probably forever bear the footnote
'*Man who offed himself because of asterisks', which would just be horrible.

Photography

I have this thing I do when I see something beautiful
I blink
and when my eyes pop back open I see the thing's
shifted
like it was betrayed by a little clink in the vast clock-
work
of things, the flux of stuff is momentarily
turned
into artwork, you know, how beauty is just better off
still.

Sometimes I blink rapidly in front of the mirror and
make
an old movie of my movements, which are usually a
jazz
handed dance and shrug of the shoulders, because
I like
to see myself clipped up, the way graffiti's seen from
the subway.

I've often wondered exactly what duration of time a photo
catches,
and does it loop that time forever, and since that time's so
minute
we don't see its short, clipped flutters, only beauty and the
semblance
of a quiet space, is a photo like a lock, hooked carefully inside
a clock?

Art

Poverty was an inflection that we all drawled
and sunk. We let our eyes fall like wrists when
we guffawed. We stank.

The miniature livelihoods of the bourgeois
were, for a time, our bread and butter, but the rascal
lower classes (ourselves

included, of course) went and met the middle-
class in the middle. These were lean days, friends.
Art recurred upon its initial

errs, and the Catholic iconography settled
like silt over the grassroots movements. Universities
filled with spit. Knowledge

and vulgarity seemed to form two smooth balls.
They reek'd of wing'd things hitherto furthermore,
if you catch my drift.

In the galleries, as in the madhouses they fathered,
pills were apportioned
by the white-coated men.

Someone was screwing Derrida with his mind,
and someone couldn't get enough of the artichokes
and the art, which looked poorer

than a loaf of bread. I built an art house out of
post-structuralism. You can guess what became
of the likely place. Falling

was, for years, the central motif in our art,
but we hit the ground last year, when
the markets crashed.

Someone was painting nudes with their speech.
Someone died, and we mixed her ashes with
oil paint and made a circle.

We all got sick from it. The New-Fascists disbanded,
power struggles we heard. And the Incidentalists
burst into flames.

A movement started on the James Bay pier—
the artists just held a canvas up to the breakwater
and waited for art to crash in.

Too many unnecessary deaths. The solipsists
made self-portraits out of their bodies, and the realists
bought them up in auctions. As for the critics,

they can wave their wands at us, and wear
itty sunglasses and that's fine, but we're
trying for something trans-

cendental here! Every generation, on the giants'
shoulders, feels compelled to bite
the back of their heads a bit. Not us.

We believe in an invisible pulley now, that
winches one over the ocean.

Poesy

You could imagine my elation, my profound pride,
upon receiving such an offer: The Paper Boys cordially inviteth you
to partaketh in a sexual renga. There on my stoop

in a Garry oak basket. I suppose that's the beginning;
the protoplasmic author burbled around its place in time. My name
came to signify the Island tabula, upon which many goodly

verses were writ, and wherein the old guard had, since
the early 1980s, baked their rustic poems about beauty.
As silver hairs grow on a lady's chin, their age somehow

signified transgression. (What wiccan herbs have they burned
to keep alive, I overheard someone whisper once at a reading.)
Love was meted out like Reichsmarks in the Weimar Republic,

ever inflating. The coffee got bitterer and more opaque,
as did the tea and beer. At the age of consent, They gave me my title—
Ivan, I was called, a 68th generation Roman—and many garrulous masks

they made me wear in order to appease the oaks. I rhymed then.
I was taught never to do so again. I remember little else
about that time: the timbre of the oaken gavels, and the geoduck ceviche

Norman Paper served me, upon returning from Central America.
I was bed-ridden for days (which Norman says was good for me—
an "experiencia" it's called in Nicaragua. Often self-inflicted too!)

From there I only got better and better. My poems
no longer began with "So," and scarcely ended with "Ta-da!"
My name corrupted upwards from legality, into a loftier stratum

where deeds are measured holistically, apart from society proper.
Upon it I flew little haiku kites and clouds of dissipating ghazal. Norm
invited me to all the Paper People orgies (the name changed in 1999,

due to complaints), within which I wore the silver crown.
Along the James Bay pier the Incidentalists wept to no avail
into the wrong end of the Pacific,

but I knew exactly what I wanted to say: something
about how the gods could take my human form, if only my yoga mat
continued to unroll, my coffee continued to steep

its tannic potential and the pier discontinued
its constant refrain. I wanted to say something
about art that had only been dreamed of,

once, by some somnambulant
sailor on his expatriation voyage—
though he never dared say it aloud.

Journalism

Brother Levi came down with a case of the "feelies"
and had to be pulled off a story, but, sorry, if you can't keep
your pants-poker holstered you can't have any word pie,
end of story.

He kept saying love life TK, 'til his two bombs had nary
a single tick left on them—kabloom, brains. His office smells
like the glue of another name's plaque being mounted now.
There's no use living between a broom and a rug, I say,

we're in it deep and scary. I've been with The Plan
for nigh on 44 years, and have seen clean-shaven stalwarts go
the way of the buffalo. The baby-making yoga has its tantric effect
on some, and poor L's cautionary tale, it fell on me to tell it.

You'll find me in the yellow pages, under 'The Case',
or through punched-out billboards on the Emily Carr highway.
I shared an office with L and witnessed
morningly his sentimentalizing the seasons,

saying, "O, aren't the leaves just like little bonbons,
or swastikas, or goose bills! Say, this coffee sure is animated today,"
which made him vulnerable to Passions and, in my opinion,
unfit to deliver the news. Every day I arrived

clothed in history's ghost, a pneumatic column of contexts
that blasts out the fingers. Levi failed to realize
this is a forever job we took. When you submit to The Plan,
it's a give-me-wisdom deal more stringent than Islam.

I look at young journalists now, dressed like train conductors,
with bygone Irish moustaches and feel an existential pain fill
the buckets in my body; if my druthers were godly powers
I'd make it rain a terrible truth.

If you've noticed my name on an article, I've failed.
I am the son of Mr. and Mrs. Inevitable and I am
a force of the most basic nature. I word. Word mean. Mean
you. You word. That's it: squeaky fucking clean.

He And I

To him the coast was a spate of seagulls discharging
their shampoo-lather shit on jetties, as skeletal as the few white crabs
the ocean had deposited at his feet, making him

a kind of crude Botticelli painting. He was born
in a hay-bale, populated by low, glutinous growth
or an acre's eighth of brassicas the colour of American

money. He didn't grow up around what I did,
the wafts of organic matter, viz., fruit flies licking clean
an accidental sockeye, nor the It's a Small World streets

of recent immigrants and old Victorians quibbling
over a low-hung oak or inch of lawn. (Always the immigrants
had the advantage of probably not dying first.)

His was a dehydrator heat, a crisper for hydrangeas;
the neighbours had it out over ground-water or choke-weeds;
Crane-flies scratched at the dry

conjunctivae of frog's eyes, on a lake where
men fought and women enjoyed cool, Worcester-heavy Caesars;
a country of cruelty and leisure. If I'm extrapolating,

I apologize. His pantomimic poems, in which cold
combs over wheat-fields, and birds look like something they aren't
never got through to me, and he told me my "word soups"

are too de rigueur and dopey to be of lasting importance.
Yet, the night intrigues us both, ah, when we could be anywhere,
when estrangements extinguish and

the sky puts on its dark underwear. We dance;
he believes that the stillness was perfect and we need heedfully to honour it, whereas I like to flail like an elephant and spit like a matted llama.

Brand New Sex Moves

I heard it from a friend of a friend,
whose son was caught
in an abandoned factory near the airport:

The kids are doing the Coq au Vin,
drenching themselves in fine Burgundy then
stuffing each other into a crock pot.

The kids are doing it like our old
mini-van, sliding at the side and smelling
of French fries.

They are doing the Salt March,
the Bay of Pigs, the Suez Crisis, three hip-thrusts
to the torso of the twentieth century.

The kids whittle dildos from orchids, pleasure
from the icy blue swoops of a social media site
only the kids know, because its sex was invented

yesterday, at 8am while they dreamed a similar
dream, a plush castle of sex moves wading
in the ether. They don't even insert half the time.

Sex to them is an infinite monkey
book of possibility, danger. The kids are doing
the improv, yes-anding each other until

the fourth wall breaks. The kids are spinning
in the purple of endless angularity, working
like hot space dust from the trauma of birth,

earning one another, spending one another,
mortgaging their bodily concepts. The kids
are doing it like two cannibals in a bathtub,

consuming each other, leaving
a perfectly satisfied void.

Ars Poetica

When the horn-god comes to tuck me back into chaos,

/when all over the James Bay pier the dying scent of chamomile
and across the street coffee and milk narratives about the boy
who did a drug and died waft in, as if from a wafting machine
/when all the plums in China ferment
/when my Greek boss, with his cassis and shank-meat breath, the
aniseed lows and alcohol vapour, and his good-hearted wife argue
/when brass looks so much like gold that I don't care
/when in Rome the Romans do as I do and press random buttons
until the thing turns on
/when the Deus ex machina is a Turbatio ex machina

And silence is unremitting, the doors are grander and less ornate,

/and the roads through downtown are palled by cotton bolls
which stick to my face
/and Chinatown looms like a question over the lower end of
Fisgard street lapping in its odd oils
/and my wrists are macerated and tattooed from trying to wait
tables while the apocalypse turns its mites up to a new pantheon
of ideals, bountifulness being the operative one
/and the battery age is knocking begging to be charged again
/and the Empress looks like it's on the fritz again
/and light 'peeks' out from the tough cumulus but I forget
what that's supposed to mean

I will read this for its poetics, so he knows the things I meant

/I will drive through the confetti showered and localized
and carve my prize into the cherry bark
/I will bundle up an incense torch and sing to the Multifarious

sung for by the dragon-men and sung to blow the fish scales
off their lips
/I will remind myself that even paychecks have parameters
/I will read Whitman to my rumpled torso, so I know
the things I meant
/I will unplug and plug I will unplug and wait and plug
and if that doesn't work I will reevaluate its honesty
/I will assure myself by tucking forward I meant the things
I meant

You Can Find the Answers on Page 56

Yet you linger. A question mark
hooks your eagerness from well within you like a wedgie.
The letters to its left, astronauts denuded of their suits,
vacuumed and suspended in the astral sneeze.
What is a four-letter word used primarily to request specification.

You flip to Page 53, almost committing, still innocent: you can find
monkeys in the Caribbean that have acquired a taste for liquor,
apparently. You shake the magazine
for a subscription card.

56 calls to you, from its summer cottage
on the right coast. Its upside-downness meant
to chasten it. Can you hear its beck over the radio,
the radio that is a question's distance from its answer, there, in a fool's
paradise of gratification only a little

delayed? You can have it all and a magazine subscription.
Go on, keep flipping past the last page. Past your lap,
through to the real monkeys drinking real daiquiris with wee green swords,
on a ruinous beach with palm trees the shape of old arms,
and answer me that.

From Your Chaise Lounge, You Poke Your Head Around Like 'What Was That?'

This is a poem that starts

This is a dig at people who wear long coats

This is a housewarming party

It's short, it's stout

This part goes like this: la la la la

I mistook a picture of Steve McQueen for George Lazemby

I like the idea of Portuguese roast chicken more than the chicken itself

This is a long relationship

This elevator is going down

This might seem odd to you, but do you have a brother in Windsor

Or a cousin

This part makes me cringe and I can't watch

I stuck to my hunch and now I'm rich

Richish

This is top gear marijuana, not at all like the marijuana in France

Or Germany

This may not make a lot of sense to you, but I'm writing from a place of near-constant regeneration now, and I've grown out of lyric

Yes, really

They make a no-name brand of orange juice as good or better than the expensive stuff

Have you stuck with it this far

Here's a treat: what do you call a joke that's also a rhetorical question

This scotch tastes like dried apricots and campfire

This is the last time I come here

I'm well respected in this area

I took a bartending course online and now I'm a prick

And other poems

You should try relaxing your eyes

This can't be understood the way you're reading it

It's really quite ingenious if you can just attach yourself to its wavelength

My podiatrist thinks I'm corny

This is the stench of a real workday

This is Peter, it's a contraction of peanut butter, his favourite food

This is life

Does Peter like a little belly scratch, does he, yes he does, yes he does

Winter

I can't seem to find the time

I stoop

This is the last perfect person

This is a window, and yonder do the children play summer games, jacketed in their future misfortunes but drinking hope through a curly straw

Winter again

You're beginning to see the meaning here

I am not

Get thee to a made bed, play your favourite music and call your friend

We've accomplished only nothing here

Sentencing

A group of my peers sentenced me
to a day culling and cataloging my important receipts
followed by a death of according inconsequence.

We had whole salmon slapping around the floor,
that's how oceanic my mother's tears were
when she found out. One judge—

bourbon barrel voice, raccoon tail
mustache—talked sweetly about the hereafter, about how
you're ferried over with nothing to carry. The other

judge was just there to be smarmy and discordant.
He had clocks behind him, and a linear model of a life
expiring on his bench. There was no executioner.

I guess they decided it was more humane to have a machine
administer the pill. Named Taxman, it had two nodes
which swapped information about crime and punishment,

according to the latest socio-ethical data. Hanging over
the execution room, portraits of the two judges flanked a detailed
Rorschach test, "*Your Life*" written in curly font at the bottom.

My father would plead to the first judge, but the second
always intervened, and what was planned took place on a rather
cloudless October day. My peers stood

watching, while Taxman held me and fed me
the dichromatic capsule, waiting only until my mourners
stopped mourning—a process lasting two whole weeks—
to pronounce me dead.

The Annihilist

> "We sit together, the mountain and me,
> until only the mountain remains."
>
> —LI PO

We sit together, the mountain and me,
until only I remain. I level its shovel-headed
top-stain, its goat-stairs, its bird-

brain. I censor the ocean's
profane abundance, its abalone apartments,
its trench coat stingrays. I stow

hope in mineshafts and fear
in rain. I do not know what the wind is trying
to say, but if I could hazard

a guess, maybe: get the flying
fuck away. Nature is as good as its
pork and cocaine. Its stars

are down-market, foreign
knockoffs of the twinkle in my eye. I could
drink its clouds in a single White Russian

and still fight a jungle with its own
teak cane. The world is old and ashamed
of its perversions; when it reflects

it comes up only with pain. I am more
benevolent, more fair and more sane. If I fall
in a forest and no one's around,

no one is permitted to remain.

For Robert

Time washed his trousers in time
and in time his deep bruises healed.

His ears grew luxuriant white
hairs appearing eminent with time.

In the wet ravines and gulches of his time-
bulbed nose in four short sneezes

he pantomimed the cross. In time
Spring set his nose going like a cuckoo clock.

He likened time once to a hooded
traveler, enjoying a slow jigger of single malt.

Time has paid its outstanding tab, tipped
its cap at the proprietor. Time

for his theoreticals to leave the bar
and brave the elements. His old body

a memorial of function, as a loose button
snoozing on a pea coat. In his backyard solarium

we hashed out my fear of death
over wine so young its soft purple bubbles

stayed dumbly where they were. You've
left for a place I fear, you who assuaged

that fear, so what do I do now? I thought
I had more time.

How to Evade Death, and Be Like the Jellyfish

Trying in my own way to become immortal, I searched
'Death' on Wikipedia, and found that one of the only species
able to evade it is the jellyfish. As the jellyfish deteriorates,
its old cells revert to a polyp state of infancy, through
trans-differentiation. Isn't this like the idea, too?
The idea, in our literature, that a single word is defined
by a series of words, each of them defining themselves
by a series of words—one large fuse box of screwy wires
firing themselves alive to make each other alive. The incest
that goes on inside a grammar dements it, evolves it inward.
The inner flux of a Shakespeare crashes wildly to us,
like squalls on a movie set, so real they're real.
Would that we were the word made flesh, the Logos
made Logical, so even in the moment of death, even
when our eyes roll back like an alligator's to evaluate the inside
parts, even when our muscles lack the definition that one
time helped them pick this rascal pen up and write this
idea, which now rolls back like the moon in wane,
night doubling, we could refigure ourselves for an inverse
function, the stuff that defines another body's life.[1]

---

[1]Would that we were the waning ones, our screwy wires
might guarantee us time to pick this pen up and write
this idea somewhere: it's it because it exists.
In our rascal literature, the likelihood of a deteriorating
Logos, the idea that one word is defined by another
word's infancy, the idea of a grammar showing up
at my door at night like, say, an alligator, to evaluate
the inside parts of it, would be equivalent to the jellyfish
expressing one of its own Shakespeare. I searched 'Immortal'

on Wikipedia, trying in my own way to become death,
but found only a demented movie set, with fuse-box polyps
and an inner squall. I found that through trans-
differentiation, the word made flux, even our muscles,
doubling themselves in incest, can refigure themselves.
Even in the moment of death, even when our eyes roll
back like the earth rolling back like the moon in wane,
this set of equivalents, evading its flesh, firing itself alive,
reverts to another value—the stuff, maybe, that a life defines.

Funeral

I remember he told me a story
from his childhood, he was following along the rope,
amid the TV static of a William's Lake winter,

tasked with feeding the horses, when he
was visited by an apparition who appeared to be
in the throes of a roaring orgasm. And,

with no one around to see him, he stopped
there in the below 30, threading his little elephant-trunk-
cock through his long johns and did the very same.

Course, he always did mimic the spirits.
And that's why I don't worry what's become of him,
whatever him was, whatever it means to become,

de-become.

I knew him in his troubadour days, sniffing
bloodhoundedly around the N. American continent,
taking voraciously in the taxonomical names

of local fauna, brewing to get cockeyed any
of the local flora, bedding anything that didn't smell as
bad as him, when he nicked his lip deep on

a Boricuan Hail-Mary dagger in the Florida
Keys, had this party trick where he blew wine
out of it, until it got infected. Then began

his quiet days.

I remember, he'd come home from the Abitibi mill
and dip his sulfur-stenching self in a tub of water he'd
added a cup of brown sugar to, so in the summer

the bees attended him, like he to his weekly
CPC (Communist Party of Canada) meetings; he met
a lot of muses there mostly in the form of Portuguese

men who liked to wrestle with him at day's end.
His father remarried in the Philippines, joined the Islamic
Separatists died of pneumothoracic collapse.

I remember he collapsed, around the very time
he was becoming the lung for Pacific poetics. Moretti
called him all the intrigue of a fencepost

marking no perimeter. He ate percocets and
watched the painfully limpid sunsets that followed
Vancouver Island like a canker of fool's gold,

although one of us always told him, you can't
live like this, not while The Boys, uh, People, rely
so heavily on you being upright. That was '78,

around when Jr. came.

I remember things being less than amicable
between he and Patience, though she had much of
her title in her, flying Jr. to the GGs,

while he remained to sexualize every corner
of his undergrad program. And that was around when Ivan.
When Ivan punctured the shell of whatever webby egg

he'd been gestating in. He was in Dominic's plane
every other Friday flying illegally to San Diego, then onto
La Paz, San Salvador, Managua. Part of a Pan-American

coke fascination.

I remember, he shaved everything but the beard. Everything.
Shit was at that time, '80, '81, starting to get seriously weird.
He attached a motor-belt to a radio dial

in Dom's airplane hangar in Sidney and
held proto-raves where everyone, even the grad students
who'd come to study him, was encouraged to shave

it all off. The whole hangar rang out with what
sounded like pigeons in a tinfoil cage. He took the guru thing
so seriously he hired a scribe and a page. Those were his

'automatic writing' days.

I remember, it got to him. The universities gradually took
his work less seriously. He was invited to be a VJ on MuchMusic,
invited to speak at the Communalist Book fair, invited to headline

the 420 rally at Victoria's Centennial Square. His book
covers looked more and more like psycho-surrealist hodge-podge
intended to whet his target audience's taste. As the internet grew,

so did pages dedicated to his work, with green fonts and black
backgrounds, cartoon devil and mushroom gifs, kneejerk analyses
of his mid-career work. When he filed the copyright suit, that was

when he was outed as 'just another suit'.

I guess it was the zeitgeist that straightened him out. He hated
that his work was being co-opted to sell bongs. Poetry had fully moved
into the universities, and its writers now wore ties and had

Master's degrees. He became a Buddhist, actually wrote some
of his best work about rural Shogun-era farmers. He had acreage
in the Gulf islands and ran a fruit winery there. Soon,

scholars were happy just studying his early and late work. Sort of
giggling when Incense Poppadoms was mentioned. Sighing when their
students brought a copy of Radiogasm to class. He taught too,

until his liver gave up.

I remember, he was the colour of an old broadsheet. Sick
as a dry bog. He couldn't even partake in his fruit wine. The smell
made him gag. No one here wants to remember the end,

it seems a waste, since he couldn't remember any of us.
I think it was Auden, on Yeats' death, who said: "hundreds will
remember this day as a day when something quite strange happened."

Or something. Let's not make too much of a fuss. He's left
enough for us for a thousand funerals. Beautiful ones. Aggravating
ones. One that shed light on this rare thing: a life that hooked

so many of us in.

ACKNOWLEDGEMENTS

Some of these poems have appeared or are appearing in *QWERTY, Carousel, The Walrus, The Puritan, The Malahat Review, ARC Poetry Magazine, This Magazine, The Collagist, Hazlitt, CV2, untethered, Grain* and *Geist.* Thanks to those editors for their confidence and support.

Thanks to those who read these poems and made them better: Kayla Czaga, Jessie Jones, Catriona Wright, E. Martin Nolan, Phoebe Wang, Bardia Sinaee, Laura Clarke, Jess Taylor, Marc di Saverio and Michael Prior.

I had an early champion in Garth Martens, who said to hell with doing fiction, kid, stick with this poetry thing. Thanks too to my professors at UVic, particularly Carla Funk, who nurtured the weirdness in my poems.

Thanks to my family: Claire, Joe, Livia and Timio for, in no small way, shaping how I think and talk. Special thanks to Settimio, my grandfather, the master of storytelling.

Thanks to Carmine Starnino for his confidence, encouragement and incisive editing. And thanks to David Drummond for a beautiful cover.

Thanks to the Ontario Arts Council, for allowing me the time to work on these.

And, finally, to the reason why everything is right in my life—Michelle, my first reader, thank you.

Carmine Starnino, Editor
Michael Harris, Founding Editor

SELECTED POEMS David Solway
THE MULBERRY MEN David Solway
A SLOW LIGHT Ross Leckie
NIGHT LETTERS Bill Furey
COMPLICITY Susan Glickman
A NUN'S DIARY Ann Diamond
CAVALIER IN A ROUNDHEAD SCHOOL Errol MacDonald
VEILED COUNTRIES/LIVES Marie-Claire Blais (Translated by Michael Harris)
BLIND PAINTING Robert Melançon (Translated by Philip Stratford)
SMALL HORSES & INTIMATE BEASTS Michel Garneau
(Translated by Robert McGee)
IN TRANSIT Michael Harris
THE FABULOUS DISGUISE OF OURSELVES Jan Conn
ASHBOURN John Reibetanz
THE POWER TO MOVE Susan Glickman
MAGELLAN'S CLOUDS Robert Allen
MODERN MARRIAGE David Solway
K. IN LOVE Don Coles
THE INVISIBLE MOON Carla Hartsfield
ALONG THE ROAD FROM EDEN George Ellenbogen
DUNINO Stephen Scobie
KINETIC MUSTACHE Arthur Clark
RUE SAINTE FAMILLE Charlotte Hussey
HENRY MOORE'S SHEEP Susan Glickman
SOUTH OF THE TUDO BEM CAFÉ Jan Conn
THE INVENTION OF HONEY Ricardo Sternberg
EVENINGS AT LOOSE ENDS Gérald Godin (Translated by Judith Cowan)
THE PROVING GROUNDS Rhea Tregebov
LITTLE BIRD Don Coles
HOMETOWN Laura Lush
FORTRESS OF CHAIRS Elisabeth Harvor
NEW & SELECTED POEMS Michael Harris
BEDROCK David Solway
TERRORIST LETTERS Ann Diamond
THE SIGNAL ANTHOLOGY Edited by Michael Harris
MURMUR OF THE STARS: SELECTED SHORTER POEMS Peter Dale Scott
WHAT DANTE DID WITH LOSS Jan Conn
MORNING WATCH John Reibetanz
JOY IS NOT MY PROFESSION Muhammad al-Maghut
(Translated by John Asfour and Alison Burch)
WRESTLING WITH ANGELS: SELECTED POEMS Doug Beardsley
HIDE & SEEK Susan Glickman
MAPPING THE CHAOS Rhea Tregebov
FIRE NEVER SLEEPS Carla Hartsfield
THE RHINO GATE POEMS George Ellenbogen
SHADOW CABINET Richard Sanger
MAP OF DREAMS Ricardo Sternberg
THE NEW WORLD Carmine Starnino
THE LONG COLD GREEN EVENINGS OF SPRING Elisabeth Harvor
KEEP IT ALL Yves Boisvert (Translated by Judith Cowan)
THE GREEN ALEMBIC Louise Fabiani
THE ISLAND IN WINTER Terence Young
A TINKERS' PICNIC Peter Richardson
SARACEN ISLAND: THE POEMS OF ANDREAS KARAVIS David Solway

BEAUTIES ON MAD RIVER: SELECTED AND NEW POEMS Jan Conn
WIND AND ROOT Brent MacLaine
HISTORIES Andrew Steinmetz
ARABY Eric Ormsby
WORDS THAT WALK IN THE NIGHT Pierre Morency
(Translated by Lissa Cowan and René Brisebois)
A PICNIC ON ICE: SELECTED POEMS Matthew Sweeney
HELIX: NEW AND SELECTED POEMS John Steffler
HERESIES: THE COMPLETE POEMS OF ANNE WILKINSON, 1924-1961
Edited by Dean Irvine
CALLING HOME Richard Sanger
FIELDER'S CHOICE Elise Partridge
MERRYBEGOT Mary Dalton
MOUNTAIN TEA Peter Van Toorn
AN ABC OF BELLY WORK Peter Richardson
RUNNING IN PROSPECT CEMETERY Susan Glickman
MIRABEL Pierre Nepveu (Translated by Judith Cowan)
POSTSCRIPT Geoffrey Cook
STANDING WAVE Robert Allen
THERE, THERE Patrick Warner
HOW WE ALL SWIFTLY: THE FIRST SIX BOOKS Don Coles
THE NEW CANON: AN ANTHOLOGY OF CANADIAN POETRY
Edited by Carmine Starnino
OUT TO DRY IN CAPE BRETON Anita Lahey
RED LEDGER Mary Dalton
REACHING FOR CLEAR David Solway
OX Christopher Patton
THE MECHANICAL BIRD Asa Boxer
SYMPATHY FOR THE COURIERS Peter Richardson
MORNING GOTHIC: NEW AND SELECTED POEMS George Ellenbogen
36 CORNELIAN AVENUE Christopher Wiseman
THE EMPIRE'S MISSING LINKS Walid Bitar
PENNY DREADFUL Shannon Stewart
THE STREAM EXPOSED WITH ALL ITS STONES D.G. Jones
PURE PRODUCT Jason Guriel
ANIMALS OF MY OWN KIND Harry Thurston
BOXING THE COMPASS Richard Greene
CIRCUS Michael Harris
THE CROW'S VOW Susan Briscoe
WHERE WE MIGHT HAVE BEEN Don Coles
MERIDIAN LINE Paul Bélanger (Translated by Judith Cowan)
SKULLDUGGERY Asa Boxer
SPINNING SIDE KICK Anita Lahey
THE ID KID Linda Besner
GIFT HORSE Mark Callanan
SUMPTUARY LAWS Nyla Matuk
THE GOLDEN BOOK OF BOVINITIES Robert Moore
MAJOR VERBS Pierre Nepveu (Translated by Donald Winkler)
ALL SOULS' Rhea Tregebov
THE SMOOTH YARROW Susan Glickman
THE GREY TOTE Deena Kara Shaffer
HOOKING Mary Dalton
DANTE'S HOUSE Richard Greene
BIRDS FLOCK FISH SCHOOL Edward Carson
THE SCARBOROUGH Michael Lista
RADIO WEATHER Shoshanna Wingate
LAWS & LOCKS Chad Campbell
LEAVING THE ISLAND Talya Rubin
INSTALLATIONS David Solway
MOCKINGBIRD Derek Webster
MODEL DISCIPLE Michael Prior
LATE VICTORIANS Vincent Colistro